AM
THE NETHERLANDS

Travel Guide Book

A Comprehensive 5-Day Travel Guide to
Amsterdam & Unforgettable Dutch Travel

♦ *Travel Guides to Europe Series* ♦

Passport to European Travel Guides

Eye on Life Publications

Amsterdam, The Netherlands Travel Guide Book
Copyright © 2016 Passport to European Travel Guides

ISBN 10: 1518797377
ISBN 13: 978-1518797378

~

All rights reserved. No part of this book may be reproduced in any form or by any electronic or mechanical means, including information storage and retrieval systems, without permission in writing from the publisher, except by a reviewer who may quote brief passages in a review. All photos used courtesy of freeimages.com, HAAP Media Ltd., a subsidiary of Getty Images.

Other Travel Guide Books by Passport to European Travel Guides

Berlin, Germany

Munich, Germany

Top 10 Travel Guide to Italy

Florence, Italy

Rome, Italy

Venice, Italy

Naples & the Amalfi Coast, Italy

Paris, France

Provence & the French Riviera, France

Top 10 Travel Guide to France

London, England

Santorini, Greece

Greece & the Greek Islands

Barcelona, Spain

Istanbul, Turkey

Vienna, Austria

Budapest, Hungary

Prague, Czech Republic

Brussels, Belgium

"Amsterdam was a great surprise to me. I had always thought of Venice as the city of canals..."

–James Weldon Johnson

Table of Contents

Map of Amsterdam..7
Introduction: How to Use This Guide..........................9
City Snapshot...11
Before You Go..12
Getting in the Mood
    • What to Read..17
    • What to Watch..18

Local Tourist Information..19
About the Airports...20
How Long is the Flight?...20
Overview of Amsterdam..21
 ★ Insider Tips for Tourists! ★................................22
Dutch Phrases For Emergencies................................27
Climate and Best Times to Travel..............................30
Tours
    • Amsterdam By Bike..32
    • Amsterdam By Boat..33
    • Amsterdam By Bus...33
    • Amsterdam By Minibus or Car.......................34
    • Special Interest or Walking Tours...................34

★ 5 Days in Amsterdam—Itinerary! ★
    • Day 1...37
    • Day 2...40
    • Day 3...43

- Day 4..46
- Day 5..48

Best Places For Travelers on a Budget
- Bargain Sleeps..................................51
- Bargain Eats....................................53

Best Places For Ultimate Luxury
- Luxury Amsterdam Sleeps...............55
- Luxury Amsterdam Eats..................57

Amsterdam Nightlife
- Great Bars in Amsterdam.................59
- Great Clubs in Amsterdam...............60
- Great Live Music in Amsterdam......61
- Great Theater in Amsterdam............62

Conclusion..64

About the Authors..................................65

Map of Amsterdam

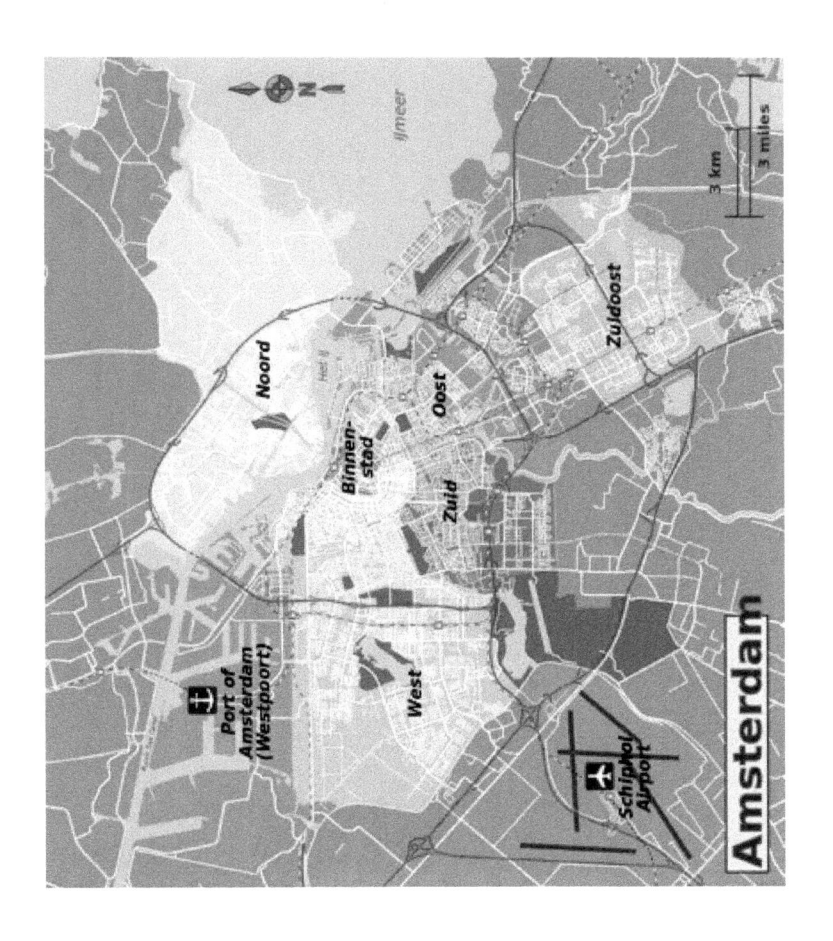

• Introduction •

Amsterdam, Netherlands. A classic and historic city with a unique urban flair. Endless canals line the cobblestone streets of the bustling, yet quaint city that is Amsterdam.

Known as the culture capital of the Netherlands, Amsterdam is filled with a vast array of activities for any type of traveler, whether it's the modern gastronomy scene or the avant-garde galleries that truly enhance any visit.

Believe it or not, this convivial city invites over 300 festivals every year with a genre variety certain to please any age of festivalgoers. **Bike-friendly paths**, canal tours and city parks provide a calming way to experience the city.

In this 5-day guide to Amsterdam, you'll find a variety of our top recommendations and helpful tips to prepare you for having the best travel experience while in the Netherlands! **Read over the insider tips** carefully and familiarize yourself with the information on preparing for your trip. Every traveler has **different**

preferences, and we've included a wide range of recommendations to suit **all tastes and budgets**.

You're welcome to follow our detailed 5-day itinerary to the letter, or you can mix and match the activities at your own discretion.

But before anything else, sit-back and know that your trip to Amsterdam is sure to be an incredibly unique experience!

Enjoy!

The Passport to European Travel Guides Team

• City Snapshot •

Language: Dutch

Local Airports: Schiphol Amsterdam Airport

Currency: Euro | € (EUR)

Country Code: 31

Emergencies: Dial 112 (all emergencies)

• Before You Go... •

✓ Have a Passport

If you don't already have one, you'll need to apply for a passport in your home country a good two months before you intend to travel, to avoid cutting it too close. **You'll need to find a local passport agency**, complete an application, take fresh photos of yourself, have at least one form of ID and pay an application fee. **If you're in a hurry**, you can usually expedite the application for a 2-3 week turnaround at an additional cost.

✓ Need a Visa?

The US State Department provides a wealth of country-specific information for American travelers, including travel alerts and warnings, the location of the US embassy in each country, and of course, whether or not you need a visa to travel there!

http://travel.state.gov/content/passports/english/country.html

Most foreigners wishing to visit the Netherlands for up to 90 days require what's known as a Schengen visa (Schengenvisum). Visitors from EU, EEA or Switzerland including a few other countries are exempt.

For more information on the specific requirements you'll need visit:

https://www.government.nl/ministries/ministry-of-foreign-affairs

✓ Healthcare

For visitors and non-residents, neither emergency nor non-emergency treatment is free. Visitors from outside Europe will have to pay for any medical services and are advised to purchase a traveler's insurance *before* traveling to the Netherlands.

Visitors from within Europe need to carry a valid EHIC (European Health Insurance Card) and present it at the time of treatment.

Should you have any minor healthcare issues (cold, flu, etc.) simply ask someone at your hotel or accommodation to point you to the nearest pharmacy (apotheek).

✓ Set the Date

July is the high season in Amsterdam, known as being one of the most crowded and most expensive months. **We suggest visiting Amsterdam** during the shoulder-seasons (late March through May, when the flowers are in bloom, and in the early fall, September and October).

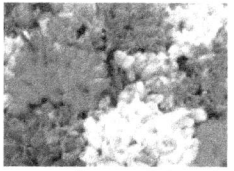

✓ Pack

The weather in Amsterdam is generally unpredictable, so learn to do as the Dutch do and be adaptable! **Pre-**

pare for changing weather with extra layers and a good waterproof jacket.

• We recommend **packing only the essentials** needed for the season in which you'll be traveling. By far, the most important thing to pack is a good pair of **walking shoes** (water-resistant if you're traveling in colder months, and comfortable, light sandals or sneakers to walk good distances in warmer months).

• If you're planning on visiting any **cathedrals or churches in Amsterdam**, be sure to pack **clothes that appropriately cover** your shoulders and legs.

• **In the colder months**, bring a **warm sweater or coat**, and a **rain jacket**. And we always recommend packing **hand sanitizer, sunscreen, sunglasses, a hat and umbrella.**

• Bring some **skin lotion** to look after your skin in dryer weather.

• **A backpack** can be handy during the day when you go out sightseeing and collecting souvenirs, particularly when getting on and off buses, boats, trains or trams.

• While many people speak English if you don't speak Dutch, be sure to pack a good **conversational Dutch phrase guide** to bring along with you. You'll find people a lot friendlier toward you if you don't go around assuming they speak your language.

• **Hand sanitizer** is always great to have along with you when traveling.

- **Medication.** Don't forget to have enough for the duration of your trip. It's also helpful to have a **note from your physician** in case you're questioned for carrying a certain quantity.

- A simple **first aid kit** is always a good idea to have in your luggage, just in case.

- You can bring one or two **reusable shopping bags** for bringing souvenirs home.

- **Travelers from outside Europe** will need to bring along a **universal electrical plug converter** that can work for both lower and higher voltages. This way you'll be able to plug in your cell phones, tablets, curling irons, etc., during the trip.

- Be sure to **leave expensive jewels and high-priced electronics at home**. Like most major cities and tourist attractions, thieves and pickpockets abound. Avoid making yourself a target.

- **Take pictures of your travel documents and your passport** and email them to yourself before your trip. This can help in the unfortunate event they are lost or stolen.

✓ Phone Home

Before your trip, add a travel plan to your cell phone bill — they're pretty inexpensive these days and will give you peace of mind that you'll always be able to phone home if need be. You can also buy a cheap, **pre-paid local phone or phone chip** for your phone — which also gives you a local phone number. Calling cards are used less and less these days, but they're also an option.

✓ Currency Exchange

The Netherlands uses the **euro** as its currency (same for most of Western and Central Europe). Check out the **currency exchange** rates prior to your trip. You can do so using **the following** or many other online currency exchange calculators, or through your bank. For the best rates, we recommend **waiting until you arrive in Amsterdam** to buy euros.
http://www.xe.com/currencyconverter

Also, make sure your bank knows you'll be traveling abroad. This way you avoid having foreign country transactions flagged and declined, which can be extremely inconvenient!

✓ Contact Your Embassy

In the unfortunate event that you should lose your passport or be victimized while away, your country's embassy will be able to help you. Be sure to give your **itinerary and contact information** to a close friend or family member, then also contact your embassy with your emergency contact information before you leave.

✓ Your Mail

Ask a neighbor to check your mailbox while you're away or visit your local post office and request a hold. **Overflowing mailboxes** are a dead giveaway that no one's home.

• Getting in the Mood •

Here are a few great books and films set in or about Amsterdam that we recommend you watch in preparation for your trip to this exciting locale!

What to Read:

Although most of us have read this worldwide classic, either in school or otherwise, this remarkable story never wanes. *The Diary of a Young Girl* by Anne Frank is an absolute must read for anyone visiting Amsterdam, where one of the most visited attractions is the city's **Anne Frank museum**. By the account documented in her diary, Anne Frank is a young girl in hiding with her family for two years in a warehouse in Amsterdam during the Nazi occupation.

One of our all-time favorite books set in the Netherlands takes place around a dinner table in one of Amsterdam's chicest eateries. *The Dinner* by Herman Koch centers on the investigation of a crime by the narrator's 15-year-old son and leaves you on the edge of your seat. This is a **continuously engaging book**; a perfect blend of politics, mystery and culture!

What to Watch:

If you saw *Ocean's Eleven* (2001) but not its sequel, *Ocean's Twelve* is set in Amsterdam with Brad Pitt, Matt Damon and George Clooney, the classic crew. The clan sets out to accomplish yet another series of heists in order to secure the funds spent on their previous theft. **With non-stop action** through the cityscapes, this is sure to get you amped up for a trip to Amsterdam!

Another excellent film is about the famous Dutch master **Johannes Vermeer**, played brilliantly in *Girl with a Pearl Earring* by Colin Firth. Set in the 17th century, and based on the novel of the same name, it's the story of a girl named Griet (Scarlett Johansson) employed as a maid in the house of Vermeer. The painter is forced to keep secret the circumstances surrounding the creation of his world-famous painting. Prep for your Amsterdam gallery jaunt by checking out this inspiring story and wonderful film!

• Local Tourist Information •

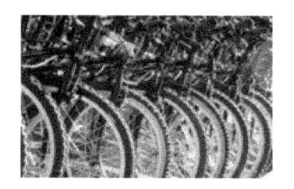

The city of Amsterdam welcomes tourists and provides much information and help to help you enjoy the numerous activities and sites the city offers. There are two official visitor centres as well as touch-screen kiosks throughout the city.

When you land, you can **pick up a free guide and map** to Amsterdam at the visitor center in the airport. Both locations sell the **iAmsterdam City Card**, which is extremely helpful in saving time and money during your visit.

I Amsterdam Visitor Center Schiphol Airport

Hours of Operation: M-F, 9:00 AM - 5:00 PM
Address: Arrivals 2 | Schiphol Plaza, Amsterdam, Netherlands
Phone Number: +31 (0) 20 702 6000

I Amsterdam Stationsplein (across from the Central Station)

Address: Koffiehuis Stationsplein, Amsterdam, Netherlands
Phone Number: +31 (0) 20 702 6000

• About the Airports •

Schiphol Amsterdam Airport lies approximately 10 miles from the city and is easily accessible by train, shuttle or taxi in about a half an hour.

On the Web:
http://www.schiphol.nl/index_en.html

• How Long is the Flight? •

The Flight to Amsterdam:

- **From New York City:** approx. 7.5 hours
- **From Chicago:** approx. 8 hours
- **From Los Angeles:** approx. 10.5 hours
- **From Toronto:** approx. 7.5 hours
- **From Moscow:** approx. 3.5 hours
- **From London:** approx. 1 hour
- **From Paris:** approx. 1 hour
- **From Hong Kong:** approx. 12.5 hours
- **From Cape Town:** approx. 11.5 hours
- **From Sydney:** approx. 24 hours

• Overview of Amsterdam •

Amsterdam is the capital of the Netherlands and lies in the province of North Holland with a population of approximately 830,000. The 17th-century Canals of Amsterdam feature proudly on the **UNESCO World Heritage list.**

Having been the home of people such as world-renowned painter **Vincent van Gogh** and celebrated Holocaust-era **Anne Frank**, the impressive museums are just one of the reasons to visit this energetic city.

Sightseeing highlights include the character and charm of surrounding neighborhoods like **Jordaan** and **'The Nine Streets'** that offer endless and unique choices of artsy cafés and shopping boutiques.

And guess what? It doesn't stop there. You can relax with a canal tour of the city, enjoy 5-star dining or a pleasant afternoon bike ride through the quaint streets.

So, get ready to uncover the hidden treasures and relish in all the exhilaration and fun this outstanding destination holds for you!

Amsterdam, here we come!

• Insider Tips For Tourists •

Etiquette

- **Greeting Etiquette:** Shaking hands on almost every occasion, whether meeting a business associate, stranger or acquaintance is appropriate in Amsterdam. Close friends may greet by air kissing three times near the cheek, customarily beginning with the left cheek.

- **Dining Etiquette:** The Dutch generally eat with a fork in the left hand and knife in right. Should you be invited to dine in a local's home, a small gift for the host (wine, flowers or a gift for the children) is appropriate.

- **Smoking Etiquette:** A tobacco-smoking law bans smoking cigarettes in public places. Amsterdam has a tolerance for buying and selling conservative amounts of marijuana. There are cannabis coffee shops about, however, keep in mind that cannabis is not actually legal and there are many **rules and regulations** governing its sale and use in Amsterdam.

Time Zone

Amsterdam is in the UTC (universal time coordinated) + 1 hour time zone. There is a 6-hour time difference between New York City and Amsterdam (Amsterdam is ahead on the clock). When it is 8:00 am in New York City, it is 2:00 pm in Amsterdam.

Saving Time & Money

• We highly recommend the **iAmsterdam City Card!** This discount pass gives you free entry to museums, free unlimited public transportation and a number of other valuable discounts and offers, allowing you to make the most of your precious Amsterdam time and money. An incredible value, you can find it at:
https://www.iamsterdam.com/en/i-am/i-amsterdam-city-card

• A great way to get around the city inexpensively is by renting a bike at one of the many rentals. We like **Mike's Bikes**:
http://www.mikesbiketoursamsterdam.com/rent-a-bike-amsterdam (**Phone Number:** +31 (0) 20 622 7970)

• We also always recommend booking your **flight, hotel accommodations, show tickets,** transportation, etc. as far in advance as possible to avoid higher prices. And if you can help it, avoid traveling during the peak tourism season, between June and August.

• **Airbnb** is a great way to discover incredible homes, rooms and even canal boats for rent! Many people find excellent prices on unique and often stylish hidden gems throughout the city. Visit:
https://www.airbnb.com

• There are also a number of **free activities** available daily. You can explore the city gardens, local markets, festivals and concerts, and even a few free museums and city tours! Visit:
http://www.iamsterdam.com/en/visiting/about-amsterdam/itineraries/amsterdam-for-free

Tipping

- **Tipping is customary in Amsterdam** but isn't always expected from locals. Tourists are, of course, another matter altogether. **Most bills include services charges,** but it is common to **leave extra change or round up** on a bill. If you feel you received above-average service, you can leave a few extra euros (but no more than 10%).

- **Taxi Drivers:** While tipping taxi drivers in the Netherlands is not very common, if your driver was efficient and exceptional, you can tip a few euros as a thank you.

- **Hotels:** A **porter** (€1/each bag) should be tipped if you have help with your luggage. For extended stays (more than 2-3 nights), it's customary to leave a couple euros per day for your **chambermaid**. Keep in mind: there is almost always a 15% service charge added to most hotel bills.

- **Restaurants:** In general, you can tip a couple of extra euros for a meal, however for good service in more upscale restaurants, you should tip 10-15% of the total bill.

- **Tour Guides:** If your guide gave an exceptionally memorable time, feel free to tip them a few euros, but there is no obligation to do so.

When You Have to Go

Luckily for English speakers, all you have to learn in order to ask for the bathroom in Dutch is: Waar is het toilet? (Where are the bathrooms?).

There shouldn't be a problem finding public restrooms in the city: cafés, museums, restaurants, shops, etc. Some establishments are for customers only, but there are public toilets throughout the city you can pay to use for about fifty cents.

The restrooms are called **badkamer** or just toilet; "Dames" for women, and "Mannen" or "Heren" for men.

Men are in luck with the number of 'kruls,' or **portable urinals** around the city. In addition, there are a few modern **paid robot toilets** in parts of Amsterdam as well.

Be aware that some of the restrooms you find may not have sinks or soap—don't forget to bring your hand sanitizers as a backup at all times when touring the city.

Taxes

The Value Added Tax (VAT) is a consumption sales tax throughout Europe. As of this writing, the standard rate in Amsterdam is 21%. Reduced VAT rates apply for pharmaceuticals, passenger transport, admission to cultural and entertainment events, hotels, restaurants and on foodstuffs, medical and books.

Visitors from outside the Netherlands may be eligible for a **VAT refund** if certain criteria are met: 1) you do not live in Amsterdam 2) obtain a tax free application from the merchant 3) you must retain your receipts and receive a tax free check stamp from customs 4) you must present these to a service refund location that issues VAT refunds 5) purchases must exceed the minimum of typically €50.

Phone Calls

The country code for the Netherlands is 31.

When calling home from Amsterdam, first dial 00. You will then hear a tone. Then dial the country code (1 for the U.S. and Canada, 44 for the UK, 61 for Australia, 7 for Russia, 81 for Japan, and 86 for China), then the area code without the initial 0, then the actual phone number.

Electricity

Electricity in the Netherlands, as in the rest of Europe, is at an average of **220-230 volts,** alternating at about 50 cycles per second (to compare, the U.S. averages 110 volts, alternating at about 60 cycles per second.) As discussed before, when traveling from outside Europe you will need to **bring an adapter and converter** that enable you to plug your electronics and appliances into **the sockets** they use.

Cell phone, tablet and laptop chargers are typically dual voltage, so you won't need a converter, just an adapter to be able to plug them in. Most small appliances are likely to be dual voltage, but **always double check** when possible, especially to avoid frying hair dryers and travel irons.

In Emergencies

The emergency number in Amsterdam is the pan-European number, 112. Emergency operators will be able to speak to you in English.

For any minor healthcare issues (cold, flu, etc.) you can ask someone at your hotel or other accommodation to direct you to the nearest pharmacy (apotheek). They're typically marked with a green cross and are usually open Monday-Friday, from 9:00 a.m. to 5:30 p.m.

For US citizens who may need governmental assistance (lost passport, etc.) you may contact the **US Consulate in Amsterdam**.

For the most current business hours visit:
http://amsterdam.usconsulate.gov/emergency_svcs2.html (**Phone Number:** +31 (0) 20 575 5309).

Dutch Phrases For Emergencies:

Ik begrijp niet.	I don't understand
Bel een ambulance.	Please call an ambulance.

Gelieve hulp te sturen onmiddellijk .	Please send help immediately.
Helpen!	Help!
Bel de politie.	Please call the police.
Ik ben ziek.	I am ill.

Holidays

On the main public holidays in Amsterdam, banks, government services and most shops and museums close earlier or entirely, but many restaurants, cafés and bars stay open.

January 1 — New Year's Day (Nieuwjaarsdag)
March 27 & 28 (dates vary) — Easter Sunday (Pasen)
April 27 — King's Day (Koningendag)
May 5 (dates vary) — Ascension Day (Hemelvaart)
May 15 & 16 (dates vary) — Pentecost Sunday (Pinksteren)
December 5 — Sinterklaas (not an official public holiday)

December 25 — Christmas Day (Eerste Kerstdag)
December 26 — Boxing Day (Tweede Kerstdag)

Hours of Operation

Restaurants in Amsterdam are often closed on Sundays and Mondays. Most will open from noon to 2:30 p.m. for lunch and re-open for dinner at around 6-10 p.m.

Banks are open Mondays thru Fridays 9 a.m. - 5:00 p.m. ATMs are available all around the city 24/7.

Museums are typically opened daily with shorter weekend hours. Be sure and double-check your travel dates for public holidays, which can change tourism hours.

Shop hours in Amsterdam are typically shorter on Sundays and Mondays with other days of the week opening much earlier and closing as late as 9:00 p.m. (Thursdays).

Post offices are usually open Monday thru Saturday 7:30 a.m. - 6:30 p.m. Bright orange TNT mailboxes can be used for sending stamped letters. For mailing being sent outside the city, be sure to use the slot marked "Overige Postcodes" (Other Postcodes).

Money

As we mentioned, the currency in the Netherlands is the **euro** (€/ EUR).

It's best not to carry more than **€150-€200 in cash** at any given time. In the event of loss or theft, this will minimize your damages.

It's best to utilize **ATMs** (geldautomaat) and tellers in the **non-tourist areas** of the city and be sure to use common sense and not make yourself a target for pickpockets. If anyone approaches you unexpectedly, it's best to politely keep walking.

Also, **beware the unnecessary fees.** If you're given the option to pay in dollars vs. euros when using your credit card, simply say no. Paying in dollars **will cost you more** in fees and you may or may not be informed of the additional charges at the time of the transaction.

Climate and Best Times to Travel

Amsterdam has an oceanic climate. As previously suggested, we think visiting Amsterdam **late March through May** and **September through October** is best. Winters can get cold, but never usually below 40F.

You can expect the **best weather** in Amsterdam from **May through September**.

June thru August is warm, very crowded and more expensive all around.

Transportation

The Netherlands has some of the best public transportation options in all of Europe. A super modern metro system, railways, buses, and excellent bike paths can move you efficiently throughout the city.

The OV-chipkaart is a public transportation card used in the city for trams, metros and buses. Metro trains run from 6 a.m. to midnight.
https://www.ov-chipkaart.nl/apply-1.htm

Licensed taxicabs have a blue number plate and are typically metallic- or black-colored station wagons. There are a number of them throughout the city.

Driving

Cycling the scenic bike routes is a must-have experience for any visitor. We recommend getting around mostly on foot or by bike.

Driving in Amsterdam can be stressful even for locals. The winding narrow roads, cycle traffic and scores of people can all be a headache to maneuver. **Parking** can be extremely expensive and difficult to find.

However, should you still decide to rent a car and drive while in Amsterdam, the Dutch do drive on the right-hand side of the road. You have to be at least 18 and have a current driver's license, passport and valid insurance.

• Tours •

Amsterdam By Bike

Mike's Bike Tours offers a variety of incredible cycling around Amsterdam and is a personal favorite of ours. Enjoy a few hours or a full day of Amsterdam's culture, history and hot spots with an English-speaking guide.

Mike's Bike Tours - Amsterdam
Address: Kerkstraat 134 H 1017 GP, Amsterdam, Netherlands
Phone Number: +31 (0) 20 622 7970
www.mikesbiketoursamsterdam.com

Joy Ride Tours is a small company that focuses on uniqueness and quality. Personalized bike tours though the city and Dutch countryside cater to families, couples and solo riders alike. The money back guarantee assures their service provides an excellent ride!

Joy Ride Tours
Address: Museumplein, 1017 MA, Amsterdam
Phone Number: +31 6 436 11 798
www.joyridetours.nl

Amsterdam By Boat

Amsterdam Canal Cruises provides an unforgettable experience cruising though the 65 miles of canals that flow throughout Amsterdam. The river cruise is an excellent way to wind down from a long day of shopping, giving you an escape from crowded and noisy sidewalks.

Amsterdam Canal Cruises
Address: Stadhouderskade 550, 1072 AE, Amsterdam
Phone Number: +31 20 626 5636
http://www.amsterdamcanalcruises.nl/index.html

Boaty has the lowest rental prices for electric boats. The boats seats up to six people and you don't need a license or experience to become captain of your own personal boat! Enjoy navigating the seemingly endless canals of Amsterdam with just your friends and loved ones.

Boaty
Address: Ferdinand Bolstraat 333, 1072 LH, Amsterdam
Phone Number: +31 6 27 149 493
http://www.amsterdamrentaboat.com

Amsterdam By Bus

CitySightseeing Amsterdam offers a 'Hop on-Hop off' bus tour that we love! There's a panoramic rooftop to enjoy all the views of the historic buildings that line Amsterdam's skyline and you can hop on and hop off at any of the stops along the route.

CitySightseeing Amsterdam
Address: Damrak 26 1012 LJ, Amsterdam
Phone Number: +31 (0) 20 420 4000
www.citysightseeingamsterdam.nl

Amsterdam By Minibus or Car

Amsterdam City Tours offers a tour that will show you the "hidden city" of Amsterdam with the ease and attention of your own personal driver. Most of what other tourists miss on a typical trip can be enjoyed with the luxury and freedom of sightseeing at your own pace with this private tour.

Amsterdam City Tours
Address: Tramplein 8A, 1441 GP, Purmerend, Netherlands
Phone Number: +800 348 7902
http://tours.amsterdamcitytours.com/details/3346/Amsterdam-City-Tour-by-private-carminivan

Try Special Interest or Walking Tours

Intrigued by the infamous Red Light District? We recommend **Local Experts Amsterdam's awesome Red Light District & Old Amsterdam** tour! They do an excellent job of taking you behind the notorious facade of the district. You'll learn about how the area came to be, daily life in the district and much more!

Local Experts Amsterdam - Red Light District & Old Amsterdam Tour
Address: Postbus 90374, 1006 BJ, Amsterdam
Phone Number: +31 20 408 5100
http://www.local-experts.com/english/amsterdam/excursions/city-walks/19/red-light-district

If you're not easily spooked, we highly recommend Amsterdam City Tours' exciting **Ghost Tour of Amsterdam!** Did you know the city's extended history has spooky legends about witches, demons and ghosts? Some places are said to even still be haunted!

Amsterdam City Tours - Ghost Tour
Address: Tramplein 8A, 1441 GP Purmerend, Netherlands
Phone Number: +800 348 7902
http://amsterdamcitytours.rezgo.com/details/28668/ghost-tour-amsterdam

Take a free walking tour of Amsterdam with **Sandeman's New Europe** and discover the unique local culture the city has to offer. Get your walking shoes on and let Sandeman's help show you the way, for free. The 3-hour tour will cover the Red Light District, Royal Palace, Anne Frank House, The Jewish Quarter and more. Enjoy!

Sandeman's New Europe - Free Tour of Amsterdam
Location: This tour starts in front of the National Monument at Dam Square

Phone Number: +49 30 510 50030
http://www.newamsterdamtours.com/daily-tours/new-amsterdam.html

Join **Local Experts Amsterdam** for a great tour of the **Jordaan quarter**, one of Amsterdam's most interesting areas! Known for being one of the most charming and romantic neighborhoods in the city, it was once one of the poorest areas of Amsterdam but today this **17th century district** is a rather chic and upscale hot spot. This tour takes you through the **hidden gems of Jordaan**, whether it be Amsterdam's oldest brown cafés, hidden courtyards and eccentric shops, or learning more about Anne Frank — we're sure you'll have a great time!

Local Experts Amsterdam - Jordaan quarter
Address: Postbus 90374 1006 BJ, Amsterdam
Phone Number: +31 20 408 5100
http://www.local-experts.com/english/amsterdam/excursions/city-walks/16/jordaan-quarter

• 5 Days In Amsterdam! •

Enjoy this 5-day itinerary for a well-balanced and easy-going experience in Amsterdam! Modify or adjust if you like! Also, be sure to **check websites or call ahead** for the most recent hours and pricing information. Enjoy!

• Day 1 •

Amsterdam has a number of things to see and many of them are doable in a 5-day period. (As we mentioned, **renting a bike** can be one of the fastest ways to get to and from the city.)

Once you arrive at the airport (always best to arrive in the morning), be sure and pick up your **Iamsterdam card** and a **free city map** at the visitor center. This will give you free access to public transportation, museums, discounts to restaurants and more.

Be sure to relax and recharge once you arrive at your accommodations. Get settled, have a nice shower and don't forget to rest and prep for any time change adjustment.

Get to know Amsterdam a bit with **Sandeman's free walking tour**—it's a perfect way to stretch your legs after the long flight (or train ride) and orient yourself a bit with the feel of the city. You'll get to see some of the highlights of Amsterdam and learn about some of its history.

Singel 404 is your ticket if **you need lunch**. Prices are great and you can enjoy a variety of freshly served food with the locals. If the sun is out, **enjoy your lunch** next to the canal with a coffee or a slice of cake—makes for a perfect lunch!

Kicking back and spending a lazy afternoon at one of the major city parks is an excellent way to recover some energy from your travels. **Vondelpark** is Amsterdam's largest and most popular park with an open theatre, ponds and a nice playground. It's in close proximity to much of the city and lies just next to the bustling Leidseplein square. Enjoy a nice cup of afternoon coffee or early dinner at one of the nearby restaurants.

If you're a foodie and want a quick layout of all the **good eats in Amsterdam**, sign up for the **Walking Dinner Amsterdam** tour, a perfect way to wind down and explore some of the dining hot spots in the city.

Most importantly, catch up on your shut-eye tonight so you're sure to kick off day two in Amsterdam refreshed and renewed!

Location Information:

Sandeman's New Europe - Free Tour of Amsterdam
Location: This tour starts in front of the National Monument at Dam Square
Phone Number: +49 30 510 50030
http://www.newamsterdamtours.com/daily-tours/new-amsterdam.html

Singel 404 (Café)
Address: 1016 AK, Amsterdam
Phone Number: +31 20 428 0154
https://www.facebook.com/pages/Singel-404/113362128727222

Walking Dinner Amsterdam
Address: Oudebrugsteeg 8 1012 JP, Amsterdam
Phone Number: +31 20 770 8953
http://english.amsterdamtour.nl/evening-programmes/walking-dinner-amsterdam-activity

• Day 2 •

Amsterdam is known for bikes. Often, they outnumber people in the city. If you're not an experienced cyclist, the busy bike paths can be intimidating at first. Today you can start with one of our recommended **guided bike tours** to get oriented with the rules and traffic with an expert that can guide you safely through the paths.

Alternatively, after enjoying a nice breakfast at your accommodations, you can head out to the Jordaan area. It's common for most tourists to miss this attractive neighborhood. It's very near the city center, but often goes unnoticed.

Here you can **walk the historic streets** lined with numerous restaurants, cafes and unique shops. It's a quaint, peaceful place to spend your day exploring some of the most scenic areas of Amsterdam. You may set out on your own, or we highly recommend booking **Local Experts Amsterdam** awesome tour of the **Jordaan quarter** for today.

For lunch, experience authentic Italian cuisine at **Caffé Toscanini**, a cozy, laid back restaurant that opened in 1985. Here they serve up homemade pastas and breads with excellent Italian wine to compliment any dish.

Today you definitely want to head over to the **Van Gogh Museum**, which houses exhibits that attract people from all over the world! More than 200 paintings, 500 drawings and 700 of Vincent van Gogh's own letters are on display! **Family friendly**, the Van Gogh museum offers wonderful art workshops for kids. They've undergone expansion and refurbishment and has extended hours on Fridays with fabulous guest musicians and DJs.

Next, you can explore Amsterdam's 65+ miles of canals with **a relaxing canal cruise**, an excellent option for families with little ones, or for when your feet are just tired from walking.

Pop over to Restaurant Greetje for a traditional **Dutch cuisine dinner** in an historic atmosphere. Raved about in *USA Today, The Guardian,* et al., dinner here is sure to soothe your appetite with large plates of some of the tastiest comfort foods!

Location Information:

Mike's Bike Tours - Amsterdam
Address: Kerkstraat 134 H 1017 GP, Amsterdam, Netherlands
Phone Number: +31 (0) 20 622 7970
www.mikesbiketoursamsterdam.com

Local Experts Amsterdam - Jordaan quarter
Address: Postbus 90374 1006 BJ, Amsterdam
Phone Number: +31 20 408 5100
http://www.local-experts.com/english/amsterdam/excursions/city-walks/16/jordaan-quarter

Caffé Toscanini
Address: Lindengracht 75, 1015 KD, Amsterdam
Phone Number: +31 20 623 2813
http://restauranttoscanini.nl/english

Van Gogh Museum
Address: Paulus Potterstraat 7, 1071 CX, Amsterdam
Phone Number: +31 20 570 5200
http://www.vangoghmuseum.nl/en

Amsterdam Canal Cruises
Address: Stadhouderskade 550, 1072 AE, Amsterdam
Phone Number: +31 20 626 5636
http://www.amsterdamcanalcruises.nl/index.html

Restaurant Greetje
Address: Peperstraat 23-25, 1011 TJ, Amsterdam
Phone Number: +31 20 77 97 450
http://www.restaurantgreetje.nl/en/index.php

• Day 3 •

Today you can head over to a few more world-famous museums! Amsterdam is home to a variety of museums including, the Anne Frank House and Rijksmuseum.

Of course the **Anne Frank House** is a must-see when visiting Amsterdam. Beware of the extensive line that can form in peak-season, though. The "house" was really a warehouse where Anne Frank's father worked on Prinsengracht 267 in Amsterdam. The young teen and her family stayed in hiding for more than two years during World War II.

Now converted into a posterity museum, the exhibition still portrays the original atmosphere — the original photographs, film images, objects and documents are displayed throughout the exhibit. The museum is also home to Anne's original diary.

An educational mobile phone app is available that walks you through various locations throughout Amsterdam with regards to Anne and her family's time in the city. For more information about the app or to download, visit:
http://www.annefrank.org/en/News/News/2012/May/App-Anne-Franks-Amsterdam

Afterward, have great pizza nearby for lunch over at **Da Portare Via**! Trust us, they serve the best coal-fired pizza in the city, hands down — yum!

Rijksmuseum is on of Amsterdam's most famous museums. **The largest museum** in the Netherlands, Rijksmuseum includes historic art from Frans Hals, Vermeer and some of the Netherland's most famous pieces. A **beautiful garden** awaits you to relax amidst the green landscapes and stroll about the sculptures at no cost.

This evening you can head on over to **Brasserie Bark** for an **incredible fish dinner**. However, if you're not a fan of seafood, there are a few other options. For those wanting to try some of the tastiest **local cuisine** in a memorable atmosphere and a **fresh menu**, Brasserie Bark is the place to be!

Location Information:

Anne Frank House
Address: Prinsengracht 263-267, 1016 GV, Amsterdam, Netherlands
Phone Number: +31 20 556 7105
http://www.annefrank.org

Da Portare Via
Address: Leliegracht 34, 1015 DG, Amsterdam
http://www.daportarevia.nl

Rijksmuseum
Address: Museumstraat 1, 1071 XX, Amsterdam
Phone Number: +31 900 0745
https://www.rijksmuseum.nl/en

Brasserie Bark
Address: Van Baerlestraat 120 | Wouwermanstraat 1, 1071 BD, Amsterdam
Phone Number: +31 20 675 0210
http://www.bark.nl

• Day 4 •

Why limit yourself to the city scope? There's a beautiful countryside just minutes from downtown awaiting you!

So after breakfast, you can take a bike tour of the Dutch countryside including windmills, cheese tastings and flowers. **Joy Ride Tours** is a smaller tour company that we really like because they focus on quality experiences with smaller groups of people.

Next, don't miss the **Stedelijk Museum**. A wonderful array of contemporary and modern artistry is featured here and it's a lovely building. The line can be pretty long here so you'll want to give yourself enough time to enjoy all that's on offer.

You can also explore some of the **brown cafés** of Amsterdam today. **De Zotte's** is an excellent place to start. Serving great Belgian beers, steaks, lamb and even tasty vegetarian dishes like quiche. It's a great place to stop for a filling lunch and even return for dinner this evening.

The Keukenhof gardens are another must see. Known as the Garden of Europe, it's one of the biggest and most magnificent floral gardens in the whole world! It truly is a sight to behold!

End the night with a bang! Dance it away at one of Amsterdam's hottest clubs. For live music you can head over to **Paradiso**, a world-renowned hot spot for the lively club atmosphere and contemporary music.

Location Information:

Joy Ride Tours
Address: Museumplein, 1017 MA, Amsterdam
Phone Number: +31 6 436 11 798
www.joyridetours.nl

Stedelijk Museum Amsterdam
Address: 5 Museumplein 10, 1071 DJ, Amsterdam
Phone Number: +31 20 573 2911
http://www.stedelijk.nl/en

De Zotte
Address: Raamstraat 29, 1016 XL, Amsterdam
Phone Number: +31 20 626 8694
http://www.dezotte.nl

Keukenhof Holland (Gardens)
Address: Stationsweg 166A, 2161 AM Lisse, Netherlands
Phone Number: +31 252 465 555
http://www.keukenhof.nl/en

Paradiso
Address: Weteringschans 6-8, 1017 SG, Amsterdam
Phone Number: +31 20 626 4521
http://www.paradiso.nl

• Day 5 •

How about sleeping in today and grabbing a semi-late brunch? Sound good?

Well, instead of eating at your hotel this morning, we recommend heading over to **Gs** for **a hearty brunch.** Known as a breakfast innovator, Gs offers a dreamy setting with delicious breakfast classics like eggs Benedict. It's day five…enjoy a **brunch cocktail!** From mimosas to bloody Marys, Gs has you covered. And if you're visiting on a weekend, you can even enjoy their **brunch cruise** through the Amsterdam canals.

After brunch, head over to Amsterdam's chicest shopping area — **P.C. Hooftstraat:**
http://pchooftstraat.nl/en

The 'Rodeo Drive' of Amsterdam is neighbor to the popular museum corner, including the Stedelijk and the Rijksmuseum. **Enjoy people watching and luxury shopping** while strolling along a variety of cafés and great local cuisine.

If the sun is out, you have to experience some of the rooftop terraces in Amsterdam. Because it's located so far north, summer months are extra long in Amsterdam…although there are many days when the sun doesn't quite make it through the clouds, so enjoy it if it does! **One of the best rooftop terraces** is located at Amsterdam's **DoubleTree Hilton Hotel**, just a short walk from the train station. Enjoy some of the **finest cocktails** in the city while soaking in some of the sunrays from the 11th floor of this panoramic hot spot.

And in case you haven't seen enough of it yet, you have to experience the electricity of Amsterdam's **Red Light District**. Pulsing with energy, this is a must-see for any tourist seeking the atmospheric quirks of this one of a kind city. It's a great day for **Local Expert's tour** of the district.

Turning off Oudezijds Achterburgwal 99 in the Red Light District onto a quiet alleyway will lead you to **Blauw aan de wal.** Here you can enjoy a three-course menu in a quiet, luxurious atmosphere with fine cuisine.

Location Information:

Gs (Restaurant)
Address: Goudsbloemstraat 91, 1015 JK, Amsterdam
E-mail: reserve@reallyniceplace.com
http://reallyniceplace.com

Sky Lounge/Bar | Doubletree Hotel - Amsterdam Centraal Station
Address: Oosterdoksstraat 4 1011 DK, Amsterdam
Phone Number: +31 20 530 0800
http://www.amsterdam.doubletree.com

Local Experts Amsterdam - Red Light District & Old Amsterdam Tour
Address: Postbus 90374, 1006 BJ, Amsterdam
Phone Number: +31 20 408 5100
http://www.local-experts.com/english/amsterdam/excursions/city-walks/19/red-light-district

Blauw aan de wal
Address: Oudezijds Achterburgwal 99, 1012 DD, Amsterdam
Phone Number: +31 20 330 2257
http://www.blauwaandewal.com/en

• Best Places For Travelers on a Budget •

Finding suitable accommodations at a comfortable price-point can be a challenge—we've got a few solid recommendations for your trip if you're on a budget. Enjoy!

Bargain Sleeps

CitizenM is our favorite bargain hotel in Amsterdam for the **boutique hotel décor**, excellent service, luxury bedding and glass toilets. The location is also good, just a short ride away from the city proper by train or tram.

Location Info:

CitizenM
Address: Prinses Irenestraat 30, 1077 WX, Amsterdam
Phone Number: +31 85 888 7230
https://www.citizenm.com/destinations/amsterdam/amsterdam-hotel

Location, location, location...The Flying Pig Uptown Hostel is an excellent choice if you want to be in an accessible area of Amsterdam, not to mention the number of other travelers you'll have the chance to meet. From private rooms to dormitories, it's your choice at attractive rates.

Location Info:

Flying Pig Uptown
Address: Vossiusstraat 46-47 1071 AJ, Amsterdam
Phone Number: +31 20 400 4187
http://www.flyingpig.nl/hostels/flyingpiguptown.php

Cocomama is a boutique hostel with sophisticated high ceilings, chandeliers and chic upscale hostel rooms. All rooms have en-suite bathrooms and the grounds include a sunny garden. We think it's a perfectly **charming place** to enjoy your time in the city without blowing your budget.

Location Info:

Cocomama Boutique Hostel
Address: Westeinde 18, 1017 ZP, Amsterdam
Phone Number: +31 (0) 20 627 2454
http://www.cocomama.nl

Bargain Eats

Unravel all the goodies at **Goodies.** Perfect for lunch or dinner, the food is full of variety and is very cost effective. Fresh and organic meals you'll enjoy. Fighting the heat? Enjoy a smoothie on their rooftop terrace!

Location Info:

Goodies
Address: Huidenstraat 9, 1016 ER, Amsterdam
Phone Number: +31 20 625 6122
http://www.goforthegoodies.nl

Getto is a **burger bar** packed with much fun! It doesn't matter who you are or where you're from, as this spot enthusiastically welcomes everyone! A fun and friendly staff serves up **unique style burgers**, such as the Dolly Bellefleur Lamb burger. Getto is sure to satisfy all unique and exciting cravings.

Location Info:

Getto
Address: Warmoesstraat 51, 1012 HW, Amsterdam
Phone Number: +31 (0) 20 421 5151
http://www.getto.nl

van Kerkwijk's small wooden tables are topped with everything from **French and Italian classics** all the way to **African and Indonesian specialties**. **With a nice terrace** to appreciate, we always enjoy the continuously changing menu here.

Location Info:

van Kerkwijk
Address: Nes 41, 1012 KC, Amsterdam
Phone Number: +31 20 620 3316
http://www.caferestaurantvankerkwijk.nl

• Best Places For Ultimate Luxury •

Luxury Amsterdam Sleeps

Our number one hotel recommendation for **ultimate luxury** in Amsterdam is the **Sofitel's The Grand Amsterdam**. In one of the oldest parts of the city, the elegant French style features modern art and sleek designs on its chic walls. Complete with a Michelin star restaurant, luxury spa, high-end bistro and more, you're sure to feel like royalty during your stay.

Location Info:

Hotel Sofitel Legend the Grand Amsterdam
Address: Oudezijds Voorburgwal 197, 1012 EX, Amsterdam
Phone Number: +31 20 555 3111

http://www.sofitel-legend-thegrand.com/amsterdam/en/index_amsterdam.php

Quiet and idealistic, the Hotel Pulitzer lies along the Amstel River. With only 79 rooms, each one is unique in its traditional furnishings and elegance. **Close to the Anne Frank House** and the Nine Streets shopping district, this hotel offers the entire sphere of Amsterdam right at your hotel doorstep!

Location Info:

Hotel Pulitzer
Address: Prinsengracht 315-331, 1016 GZ, Amsterdam
Phone Number: +31 20 523 5235
http://www.pulitzeramsterdam.com/en

The Intercontinental Amstel Amsterdam lies on the banks of the charming Amstel River. Opened in 1867, this elegant hotel features 55 guest rooms and 24 suites all elegantly designed and furnished. **Enjoy fine dining at La Rive**, one of only a handful of Michelin-starred restaurants in Amsterdam.

Location Info:

Intercontinental Amstel Amsterdam
Address: Professor Tulpplein 1, 1018 GX, Amsterdam
Phone Number: +31 20 622 6060
http://www.ihg.com/intercontinental/hotels/gb/en/amsterdam/amsha/hoteldetail

Luxury Amsterdam Eats

Hotel Okura houses the delightful **Ciel Bleu**, a two Michelin star restaurant. A classical setting, this immaculate restaurant **serves seasonal food**, all with local and fresh products, from caviar to king crab. From its 23rd floor perch, enjoy dinner with a breathtaking panoramic view of the city.

Location Info:

Ciel Bleu
Address: Hotel Okura, Ferdinand Bolstraat 333, 1072 LH, Amsterdam
Phone Number: +31 20 678 7450
https://www.okura.nl/en/culinary/ciel-bleu-restaurant

Bridges is one of our favorite upscale dining locales. Local ingredients and fresh seafood make up incredible fish dishes as well as fine meats and poultry options. Located in the lush **Sofitel Grand Hotel Amsterdam**, this restaurant has a mouth-watering menu sure to satisfy any distinguished appetite.

Location Info:

Bridges
Address: Oudezijds Voorburgwal 197, 1012 EX, Amsterdam
Phone Number: +31 (0) 20 555 3560
http://www.bridgesrestaurant.nl/en

This swanky restaurant in the Intercontinental Amstel Amsterdam Hotel frequently nourishes the selective appetites of royalty and rock stars, however, anyone can reserve one of the highly sought after tables at **Restaurant La Rive**. Elite travelers can enjoy an incredible dining experience of **Mediterranean and French cuisine** accentuated by impeccable service.

Location Info:

Restaurant La Rive
Address: Professor Tulpplein 1, 1018 GX, Amsterdam
Phone Number: +31 20 520 3264
http://www.restaurantlarive.nl/en

• Amsterdam Nightlife •

Great Bars in Amsterdam

SkyLounge Amsterdam is our favorite bar in the city. Cruise up to the top floor to enjoy the incredible panoramic views of the city from the terrace. Global travelers alike meet and mingle over superb cocktails, fine wines and delicious bites. The energy in the evening is spiked with great DJs turning this hot spot into a choice lounge club for a great evening out.

Location Info:

SkyLounge Amsterdam
Address: Oosterdoksstraat 4, 1011 DK, Amsterdam
Phone Number: +31 20 530 0875
http://www.skyloungeamsterdam.com/en

Named for James Bond's love, the **Vesper Bar** fashionably sports James Bond memorabilia in an atmosphere that definitely pops. With a stylish and quiet location just off of the Haarlemmerstraat shopping street, this award-winning joint will have you coming back for more.

Location Info:

Vesper Bar
Address: Vinkenstraat 57, 1013 JM, Amsterdam
Phone Number: +31 20 846 4458
http://www.vesperbar.nl

Great Clubs in Amsterdam

Sugarfactory offers a vibrant clubbing atmosphere of hot DJ's, live musicians, singers and more. The music genre is thick in a wide variety of everything from electro to techno. Don't miss this spot!

Location Info:

Sugarfactory
Address: Lijnbaansgracht 238, 1017 PH, Amsterdam
Phone Number: +31 (0) 20 627 0008
https://www.sugarfactory.nl

An electro music mecca, **Studio 80** hosts wonderfully innovative DJs, making it one of the hottest nightclubs in the city. Located in the center of Amsterdam, you can enjoy live bands, DJs, music producers and more within a smaller venue that's sure to foster a great time!

Location Info:

Studio 80
Address: Rembrandtplein 17, 1017 CT, Amsterdam
Phone Number: +31 (0) 20 521 8333
http://www.studio-80.nl

Great Live Music in Amsterdam

Our favorite spot for live music in all of Amsterdam is at Paradiso. People flock from all over the globe to catch live music from one of the most well known nightclubs in the Netherlands. Opened since 1968, Paradiso offers incredible acoustics and internationally renowned artists.

Location Info:

Paradiso
Address: Weteringschans 6-8, 1017 SG, Amsterdam
Phone Number: +31 (0) 20 626 4521
http://www.paradiso.nl

When it comes to jazz and blues, Bourbon Street's got you covered. For over 15 years, some of Europe's most talented musicians have played for guests at this **elite jazz club**. Jazz, blues, soul and funk tunes will entertain you until the later hours every night until near dawn.

Location Info:

Bourbon Street
Address: Leidsekruisstraat 6-8, 1017 RH, Amsterdam
Phone Number: +31 (0) 20 623 3440
http://www.bourbonstreet.nl

Great Theatre in Amsterdam

Amsterdam's famous Philharmonics is called **Concertgebouw** (concert building). The 19th century building serves as home to their orchestra as well as the Dutch Philharmonic Orchestra and others. Classical music is played here for an audience of over 800,000 annually, making this concert hall the second most popular in the world!

Location Info:

The Royal Concertgebouw
Address: Concertgebouwplein 10, 1071 LN, Amsterdam
Phone Number: +31 900 671 8345
http://www.concertgebouw.nl/en

One of the world's most stunning movie theatres, Amsterdam's **Pathé Tuschinski** hosts a blend of cinematic styles. Book private or balcony seats in advance and enjoy the incredible decor of this enjoyable, impressive theatre.

Location Info:

Pathé Tuschinski Amsterdam
Address: Reguliersbreestraat 26-34, 1017 CN, Amsterdam
Phone Number: +31 900 1458
https://www.pathe.nl/bioscoop/tuschinski

• Conclusion •

Offering you a taste of intense culture and friendly people, Amsterdam is undeniably one of the most unique cities in all the world. We hope you feel **inspired and motivated** to enjoy all that it has to offer!

We hope you have found our guide to the **colorful city of Amsterdam** helpful and wish you a safe, exciting and fun-filled trip to the Netherlands!

Warmest regards,

The Passport to European Travel Guides Team

Visit our Blog! Grab more of our signature guides for all your travel needs!
http://www.passporttoeuropeantravelguides.blogspot.com

★ **Join our mailing list** ★ to follow our Travel Guide Series. You'll be automatically entered for a chance to win a **$100 Visa Gift Card** in our monthly drawings! Be sure to respond to the confirmation e-mail to complete the subscription.

• About the Authors •

Passport to European Travel Guides is an eclectic team of international jet setters who know exactly what travelers and tourists want in a cut-to-the-chase, comprehensive travel guide that suits a wide range of budgets.

Our growing collection of distinguished European travel guides is guaranteed to give first-hand insight to each locale, complete with day-to-day, guided itineraries you won't want to miss!

We want our brand to be your official Passport to European Travel — one you can always count on!

Bon Voyage!

The Passport to European Travel Guides Team

http://www.passporttoeuropeantravelguides.blogspot.com

www.ingramcontent.com/pod-product-compliance
Lightning Source LLC
LaVergne TN
LVHW012330200125
801696LV00039B/1444